FARM CHARM

In the BARN

by Pearl Markovics

Consultant:
Beth Gambro
Reading Specialist
Yorkville, Illinois

Contents

BEARPORT PUBLISHING

New York, New York

In the Barn

Look around.

What do you see?

I see pigs in the barn.
Oink, oink!

What do you see?

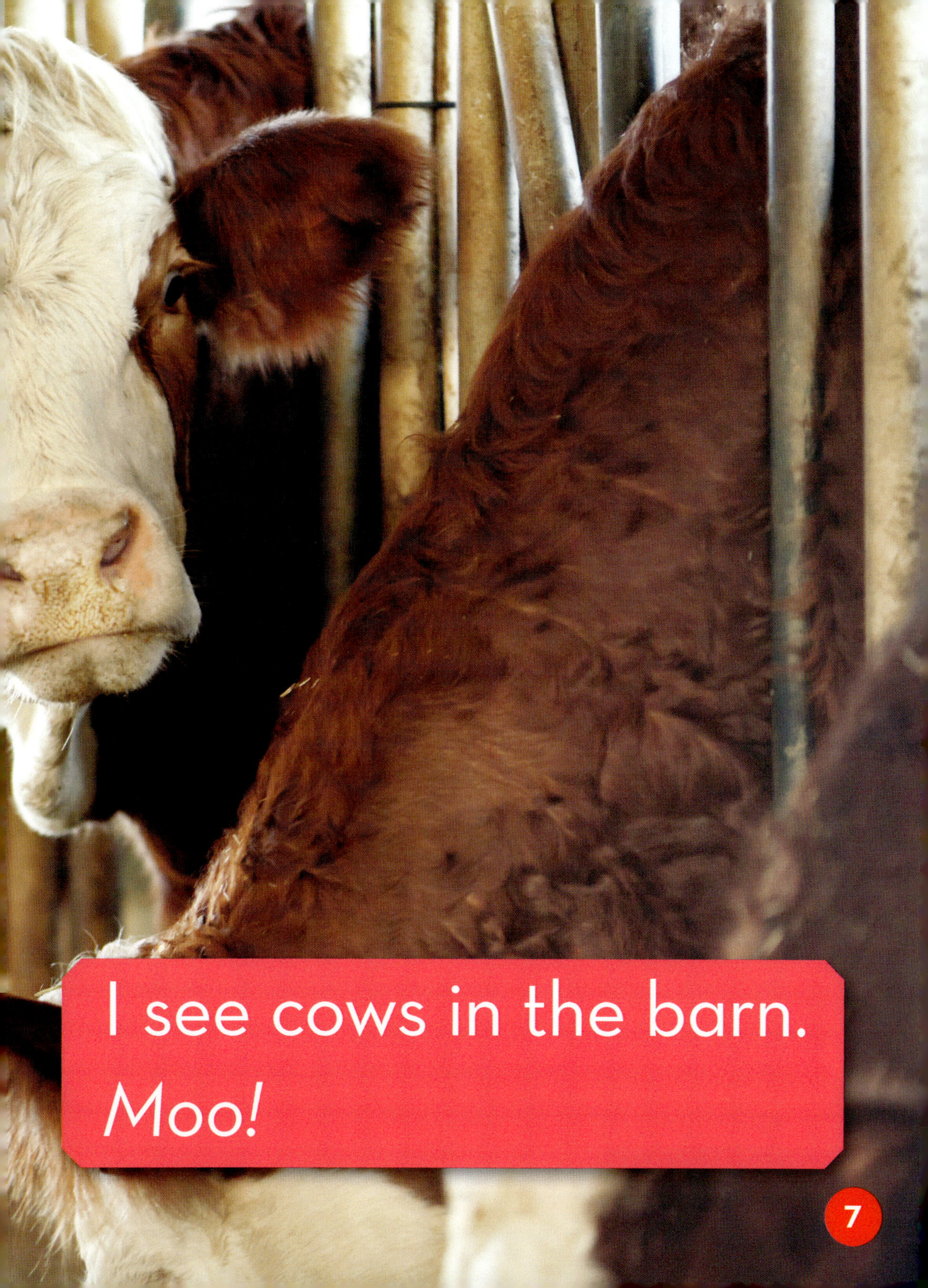

I see cows in the barn.
Moo!

What do you see?

I see sheep in the barn.
Baa, baa!

What do you see?

I see horses in the barn.
Neigh!

What do you see?

I see goats in the barn.

Maa, maa!

Look closely!

What do you see in the barn?

Key Words

cows

goats

horses

pigs

sheep

Index

About the Author

Pearl Markovics grew up on a small farm in New York. She enjoys caring for animals and stacking hay bails.